Survival Academy by Debbie Forney is a compelling read. This book is the story of a young girl whose heart was wrapped up in worldly treasures and whose moral compass was compromised by the great deceiver, Satan. In her quest for finding true love, she painfully experienced heartache after heartache until she found her faith and love in Jesus. I believe that God will use this powerful testimony to bring Glory to His name and lead others who need strength and encouragement to break away from the bondage of Satan and turn to Him.

How many times in life do we find ourselves in a situation where the only thing we can say is, "God, help!" Life can be hard, overwhelming, and a total mess in spots. This is most evident when we want to control life on our terms and attempt to shut God out. Deb opens her heart and her life as a testament to an all-powerful, merciful, and loving God who works in the midst of loss, painful choices, and broken relationships.

If you want to know how to be forgiven, forgive yourself and see relationships healed, then this is for you. The love of Jesus Christ is woven into the fabric of Deb's life. You'll be amazed to see just how, as you experience life in her shoes from her childhood at Mooseheart to her loving family today.

D1398837

When I saw the word "Mooseheart", I was hooked. Then I read more of the rollercoaster ride Debbie has been on since childhood. Her story shows the grace of God in a real, raw way. Thanks for being a good steward not just of the good, but the painful things in life.

— *Chris Fabry, Author*
Host of Chris Fabry Live
Moody Radio, Moody Bible Institute
Chicago, Illinois

Survival Academy is a call to encounter God's heart. Debbie Forney shares how she discovered a new depth of God's love amid considerable hardships. Her life story is one of healing and transformation through the grace of God. Debbie finally found her intended identity as a daughter, who is loved and enjoyed by her Heavenly Father. Her inspiring journey will tenderize and renew hearts, while instilling a determination to walk in freedom and liberty.

— *Mike Bickle, Director*
International House of Prayer
Kansas City, Missouri

I met Deb almost four decades ago and we've shared many life seasons. I've watched her diligently seek personal healing, as she unpacked her childhood story and family history with courage and determination. Deb continues to be an encouragement to everyone around her, as she allows each life experience and relationship to be a part of her transformation. Her determination and fortitude inspire me in my own God journey. I'm thankful for her transparency and vulnerability with all of us. I love you Deb.

— *Sherry McGowan, Director,*
Visiting Angels
Crystal Lake, Illinois

Survival Academy is the amazing story of Deb Forney's rollercoaster journey, in which she shares the vital lessons she learned in the process of surviving incredible and painful experiences as a very young orphan and continuing into adulthood. Deb opens her heart in the most vulnerable way, sharing her failures and weaknesses, as well as the extreme blessings she received along the way. Her story truly touched our hearts and brought tears to our eyes. Although no two stories are alike, we know many people will totally identify with much of the pain she experienced and survived. What she learned from those experiences is now being used to help others, and to give glory to her Heavenly Father, whom she has come to know in a very intimate way. This book is a very easy read, and we know it will touch your heart and greatly encourage you on your own life journey.

— *Ben R. Peters, Author, and Brenda Peters*
International Speakers
Founders of Kingdom Sending Center
Genoa, Illinois

I'm pleased to commend Deb Forney's story of finding the Father's love, as she's recounted in this little book. My own heart was touched again, as I read Deb's account of how the Holy Spirit has directed her life from very difficult beginnings, along a strenuous journey, towards discovering and becoming settled in the love of God. As you read, I pray your heart will be moved with a deeper appreciation of God's sovereign work in leading us into the knowledge of who He is, and who we are to Him. Blessings on you as you encounter God's love through Deb's story.

— *Gary Wiens*
Burning Heart Ministries
Gig Harbor, Washington

Debbie tells her story as it was lived … with the threads of God's care, love, grace, and forgiveness pursuing her in the heartache of what happened to her as a child, and as a result of her own choices. With the brokenness in the world pressing in on her, a strong survival instinct kept alive the longing to know and experience God's genuine love

Reading her story will inspire you and will challenge you to love those in broken places in ways that express the very present love of Christ. I have listened to her story and believe that you will want to have her come in person and share her story of God's relentless love … that is His desire for each of us to know.

Survival Academy

One Orphan's Life Story
and Her Search for Love

Debbie Forney

Survival Academy

© 2018 by Debbie Forney
debbieforneyinfo@gmail.com
www.debbieforney.com

Front cover photo by Laura
Front cover model: Selah Camp

*I dedicate this book
to Mooseheart,
my childhood home,
my classmates,
teachers,
coaches,
and to all who helped raise me
and cared about me
the best they knew how.*

Contents

Acknowledgements

My husband Ron ... You've loved me for better or for worse, and you've been my greatest cheerleader!

My daughter Laura ... You've been one of God's greatest gifts to me. What an amazing, talented, beautiful inside and out, young woman you're becoming!

My sisters Karen, Pam, Marg, and Dodie and my brothers Bob, Don, and Dan ... We survived and I'm thankful to call you family.

Jill Mursewick ... You came alongside me and lifted me out of the pit. Thank you for seeing my potential! I'll forever be eternally grateful for your kindness, wisdom, and friendship!

Sherry McGowan ... You showed me unconditional love and friendship from the very first moment I met you in April of 1982. You're an incredible person and lover of Jesus!!!

Mike Bickle ... Thank you for loving Jesus and for inspiring me to go deeper in my faith!

Carole Robbins ... Your ability to tighten paragraphs, re-move overused words, and polish my story, so readers can enjoy it, has been a gift. Thank you for saying "Yes" to this project. God has used you more than even you know!

Willow Creek Church ... A place where I found community and truly learned about God's love.

Moody Bible Institute ... Provided the opportunity for me to have a college education and to grow in my knowledge of God's Word. I'm also thankful for Moody's radio programing, which showed me the way back home when I'd lost my way.

Every orphan and to those who have ever felt abandoned, betrayed, or rejected, by those they looked to for love ... As you read my life story, may you also find that love, hope, peace, strength, and guidance you need through God our Heavenly Father.

And to my Abba God ... The only Father I've ever known.

Preface

I DON'T REMEMBER EITHER OF MY PARENTS, but I honor them. What I do know about them, I learned from my older siblings, other relatives, and ancestry quests. I'd like to provide some insight into who my parents were, because it might clarify what transpired in my family.

My Mother

My mother Isabel had a very short, hard life. Born in 1930, she was the youngest of three children. Her older brothers Edward and Willard were identical twins and three years old then. Her parents were both visually impaired or blind. At the time of her birth, her father Isaac was 61 and her mother Edith was 39. That certainly explained a lot. What was it like being raised by older parents who were both blind? I'm sure there were many challenges, and I have considerable empathy for my mom.

I've heard many stories about how fun my mother was, but she grew up way too fast and wanted to get out of the house. At 15, she fell in love, got pregnant, and then married. Her first son Daniel was born in 1946 when she was 16. She was very young and unable to care for him, so her husband's family raised him. That marriage eventually ended in divorce.

At 19, she met and married another man and had a daughter with him. My sister Karen was two when that marriage fell apart.

At 22, she was briefly married to a man named Steiner Geiger, but they had no children. In 1955, my mother Isabel met Robert (Bob) Lee Lehman who later became my father.

My Father

My father Bob was the firstborn of six children. He was a fun-loving man, who others described as a charismatic gypsy. He was literally a "give you the shirt off his back" kind of guy.

My dad's first wife died in 1949, leaving him with four children. He briefly had a second wife named Willodean, with no other children involved.

My dad married my mother when she was 25, making her an instant stepmother. Their relationship was rocky at best. Obviously, if they'd known any better, they would've done better. Due to unforeseen, tragic events, two of my sisters and I were introduced to Mooseheart, and so the story begins.

Reconciling Truth

I harbor no unforgiveness or judgement. I did have to release the shame that I'd carried all those years. Somehow, I'd thought that everything was my fault, and I never wanted that truth to come out. There was a wide chasm between what I believed as a child and the truth. But Jesus said, *"Then you will know the truth, and the truth will set you free"* (John 8:32). Now, I'm truly free!

Introduction

Mooseheart

Twelve Thousand Lives Made Better

MOOSEHEART HAS BEEN A HAVEN FOR CHILDREN in need for 105 years. It's a private children's home dedicated to the protection of children whose parents had died or could no longer care for them. Unlike an orphanage, these children aren't available for adoption.

Since I was only four when I arrived at Mooseheart, I had no idea how spacious and beautiful my new surroundings were. To better inform the reader, I've included a very brief history and some significant facts about Mooseheart:

- The founder of Mooseheart, James J. Davis, was revered. We honor and respect him for all that he did to make our lives better. As you drive through the gates, a large bronze statue of him surrounded by children is one of the first things you'll see.
- James J. Davis became a member of the Loyal Order of

Moose. It was with the over 400,000 members of this fraternity that he shared his vision of building a home and school for the orphaned children of its members.

- The initial 1,023 acres was purchased in 1913 for $264,000.
- The name "Mooseheart" was agreed upon, and on July 27, 1913, the "Child City" was officially opened.
- When the ground was broken, Rodney Brandon was accredited with building Mooseheart. He played a key role in guiding the campus planning, construction, and staffing it for the first three years.
- Mooseheart currently covers 1,000 acres:
  - » 313 acres are devoted to the campus and parks,
  - » More than 100 buildings, including 30 different student residences built to look like family homes, are on campus,
  - » Eventually, it became a self-contained city, with its own post office, school, hospital, farm, and power plant, and
  - » There's a picturesque 23-acre lake on the property.
- Mooseheart's original admissions policy remained largely unchanged through the early 1960's, only permitting admission to children of male Moose members who had died. As society swiftly changed between the 1960's and 1980's, Mooseheart adjusted in response. More and more children were being accepted whose families were in disarray, due to divorce, substance abuse, severe economic reversal, or other reasons. Until 1994, however, admission generally required that there be a Moose member in a child's extended family. But that year, the

Moose fraternity leaders voted unanimously to expand the admissions policy to consider applications from any family in need, regardless of Moose-member affiliation.

Two of Mooseheart's greatest architectural achievements included:

- The completion of the magnificent "House of God". Every Sunday, from the time I arrived at Mooseheart until I left, was spent learning about God in this beautiful place.
- The Mooseheart Field House, which is home to the Red Rambler Football Team and all other sports. To live at Mooseheart, you learned to love the game of football, at least I did, and I couldn't wait for the season to begin.

Please go to *www.mooseheart.org* to learn more about Mooseheart's incredible history and how you can help the children living there today!

Memories of Mooseheart

My daily life at Mooseheart would've been described as structured with lots of school, music practice, chores, homework, and play. Sounds normal, right? To me it was, because this home was all I'd ever known.

Since I was one of the "lifers", which are kids who started out in "Baby Village" and grew up in "Child City", I guess you could say that I carried some seniority. I learned how to function in this communal setting where everything you did had the potential of affecting someone else. If the weekly assignment was making toast for 12-16 girls, you didn't want to burn it, or the comments would start coming. Everything we did was up for criticism or judgement, which usually ended up with a shot being taken at our character or temperament.

We all had to function within a group consciousness, even when making decisions like what we would watch on TV for one hour each evening. We all wanted to watch *The Brady Bunch*, and most of us liked shows that had TV dads in them like Robert Reed, Michael Landon, Andy Griffith, and Danny Thomas. These actors were the closest thing we had to a father figure, because there were no housefathers taking care of us, only housemothers.

I learned a lot about resolving conflict with my dormmates, but probably not in the best way possible. Wearied by all the drama, the housemothers would tell us to, "Go back outside and work it out!" We didn't have healthy relationship skills, so we ganged up on, ignored, alienated, and made the girl we were fighting with feel horrible. When we couldn't stand it any longer, we all made up and functioned as a group again. The fact that we seldom had a break from each other says a lot about our ability to adapt and blend our assorted temperaments. Imagine going to school with the same girls you walked home with and lived with! I can say that my "sisters" growing up at Mooseheart will always hold a special place in my heart, because of our unique trauma and shared experiences.

Cleaning Chores

Cleaning was a huge part of our lives growing up. As early as four, I remember making my bed and helping to clean up our toys. In the elementary years, we were put on a three-week rotation. Those duties included scrubbing kitchen floors; washing, rinsing, or drying dishes; dusting the living room; collecting towels; scrubbing toilets; or emptying trash cans. You name it, we did it. Since our halls were open to the public, the main floors received an extra special cleaning. We had Saturday assignments that sometimes involved stripping, waxing, and buffing the floors. To accomplish these tasks, we tied rags to our feet, we danced the "twist", and we ran up and down the long, spacious hallways. The rags on our feet and all the activity made the floors shine like glass.

Creating Fun

We had to create our own fun together. We were sent outside almost every day after school for an hour and a half, until the evening whistle blew at 5:30. This steam whistle announced every part of our day; it was the long, last blast at 9:30 that meant everyone went to bed.

Winters can be very frigid, snowy, and windy in the Fox River Valley, which is 38 miles west of Chicago. It was rural, with lots of cornfields, and there was seldom a break from the relentless cold. Once again, we adapted and took great comfort, as we huddled together and took turns sitting on the manhole covers. The hot steam escaping would warm our mittens and bottoms, so we were able to play outside longer until suppertime. I'll always be grateful to God that I loved the outdoors and nature. It made growing up in my environment very enjoyable.

Being "Special"

Discipline was something that none of us escaped. They called it "special". Depending upon what the offense was, you'd receive so many hours that had to be worked off either after school or all-day Saturday and/or Sunday. When I was called to the dean's office, I knew it wasn't a social visit; it meant punishment. I was in trouble a lot.

The Dean of Boys would occasionally be called in to convey his displeasure, although I never knew how to take him. He would always start out so friendly and kind, but the sentence was always handed down in the end. I received 25 hours for chewing gum, talking in class, holding hands with a boy, and being late to class. On our favorite show, *The Brady Bunch*, when Marsha Brady wore a mini skirt, some of us, along with others in my sister Pam's class, cut our skirts short and sauntered to school. It was fun, until the punishment was handed out. Sometimes I had so many "special" hours that I felt I'd never finish them!

Visiting Moose Members

During my years at Mooseheart, there were thousands of Moose members who arrived in buses on Sundays to tour the grounds and check us out. I can still smell the exhaust fumes and hear the loud engines rumbling down our tree-lined streets. They'd stop at points of interest, seeing where their donations were being spent. I felt super special in a weird way, as we were always dressed in our Sunday best for those visits. Being a tomboy, I couldn't wait until visiting hours were over, so I could tear off my fancy dress with the layers of itchy crinoline and those uncomfortable patent-leather shoes. As I got older, I started wondering how I could get on one of those buses as a guide. In the 8th grade, I became a student guide and I loved it! The best part for me was when couples would ask me questions, and I received individual attention. I learned as much as I could about the architecture of many of the older buildings, but mostly, I was just a ham on the microphone! I talked and talked and seeing their smiles was just so great! When the tour was over, there'd always be some money slipped into my hand. I did make an hourly wage too, but the extra money helped make my checking account grow.

Celebrity Visits

There were also celebrities who came to Mooseheart to entertain us and raise money. In 1963, when I was in kindergarten, Jerry Lewis put on a show when his movie *The Nutty Professor* debuted in theaters. My grade sat in the first row, and I remember this wild, loud, lanky man laughing, getting off the stage, and heading straight towards me! He said hello and then proceeded to pick me up and tell me how pretty I was. All I remember about him was his cigarette breath and greasy hair. I cried and wanted to get down; because quite frankly, I didn't know him, and his loud-screaming voice scared me. He was just trying to be nice, but that's how things were as children of Mooseheart. They used us to tug on the heartstrings of people, so they would donate.

Family Visits

Growing up, my entire world revolved around Mooseheart. However, we were permitted to leave the campus on Sundays with our guardian(s) for the day, which meant I could spend time with my grandma, sister Marg, or brother Bob.

One of my favorite memories was the year my birthday fell on Easter. I was 10 and Easter was April 10th. That's what we called your "golden birthday", After church, we all gathered on the playground for the Easter-egg hunt. I remember running like crazy to find one of the prize eggs, and I found a large egg wrapped in gold foil under a bush! My heart was beating very fast, as I brought it to the adults in charge. Not only was it my golden birthday, I had also won something with a golden egg! Much to my delight, the prize was a huge, solid milk-chocolate bunny! I dreamt about eating it all by myself, but when I got back to my dorm for lunch, the housemother took it and said that I needed to share it. That bunny got chopped up into many pieces; but truthfully, I didn't mind. I enjoyed the candy eyes and all the girls were happy. Sharing was drilled into our heads very early in our training.

My brother Bob was married by then, and they would come to Mooseheart to get Pam and me for the day. We had so much fun! He and his wife took us on a little shopping spree and bought us each the cutest two-piece bathing suit! I also got a new dress, shoes, and a hat that I loved. I never wanted that day to end! Judy, my sister-in-law, made me a bunny birthday cake. We laughed when I told her the chocolate-bunny story; so of course, we had to chop those ears off too! When the day was over, I savored each minute of that day, because of how special I felt.

Seasonal Experiences

Mooseheart was steeped in tradition, so I had many seasonal experiences to look forward to growing up. Two that come to mind were bicycles and ice skates. Every spring, the bicycle man would ride around to all our dormitories and deliver a bicycle to every child. They were all used, but as we grew and needed a bigger one, it would be provided. Then each fall, the man who brought the bicycles took them back to a shop and got them ready for the following spring. Shortly after I turned five, I remember learning to ride a two-wheeler with all my dorm sisters watching. I was very proud of my achievement!

In the winter, we would go to a large room where rows and rows of ice skates were kept. They always gave us skates that were a little bit larger, because we wore two pairs of warm socks, so we could stay at the outdoor rink longer. When we got tired or cold, we could duck into the ice house to warm up. There were layers and layers of soft hay on the floor, and benches lined every wall. What fond memories these were!

Christmas at Mooseheart

Christmas was always one of my favorite holidays growing up. I loved hearing the Christmas carols, I enjoyed the special foods and desserts, and I particularly relished the anticipation of Santa coming! The Christmas Eve Service was spectacular! Can you imagine 600 kids sitting there all wiggling, waiting for the pastor to say "Amen", so they could run back to their halls and open the one gift that Santa had brought? No child at Mooseheart ever went without a gift or two, thanks to the women of the Moose's Christmas in October gift drives all over the country. We also had a competition for the best decorations from hall to hall, and the teachers and other staff would judge our homemade decorations. Of course, there was some bribing with cookies and other holiday treats. The winners usually had a day on snowmobiles or a pizza party. I enjoyed these times so much!

Camp Ross

We attended Mooseheart's Camp Ross every summer for two weeks. It was an hour west of Mooseheart in beautiful Mt. Morris, Illinois. I loved it there! The staff and counselors planned so many fun activities for us, and my memories of there are vast … learning to dive off a diving board, 5 A.M. polar bear swims, cooking some of our meals on an open fire, and telling ghost stories around a crackling fire. One morning, we took one of our counselor's bras. We ran out to the flag pole, hooked it on, and up it went. I'll never forget the look on the director's face when, instead of seeing the American flag and our camp flag, there was a bra flapping in the wind! I think I missed swimming that afternoon, but the story at dinner that night was worth it!

We mostly ate in the mess hall, and I remember having bug juice and other foods with crazy names, which just made them taste better. My favorite part of camp was the bus trip with all the traditional camp songs, which we sang all the way there and all the way home!

Shaped by Mooseheart

I'm thankful to have had so many special teachers, nurses, and a few housemothers growing up who genuinely cared about me! I really did have a very good childhood. We were very sheltered and had no clue about what was going on in the "outside world". But I wouldn't trade my upbringing for anything! Mooseheart shaped me and made me who I am today, and God is using everything I experienced to encourage you!

Happy reading!

Chapter 1

Orphaned Too Soon

I WAS TOO YOUNG TO REMEMBER, but I think that was a gift from God. I was the youngest of seven children. There was a blend of five girls and two boys, as the result of several marriages by my parents. By the time my mother had me, my parents' lives were in chaos, due to alcohol, unhealed wounds, and their own crazy decisions. At four, I was mostly being cared for by my oldest stepsister Marg who was 16.

My mom and dad died within three months of each other. My mother died at the hands of my father when he accidently killed her in a fit of rage. The strange part about her death is that for my entire childhood, I'd believed she committed suicide, which was the cause given on her death certificate. When I turned 21, our oldest sister Marg called a meeting. She told us what she'd witnessed the night of my mother's death, and she believed that our father had accidently killed her. Honestly, it doesn't matter anymore. Three months later, my father was in a car accident, which was one of many. When he checked himself out of the hospital, he ended up dying from complications of a cerebral hemorrhage at home. The only memories I had of my parents were associated with the scent of flowers at their funerals.

Upheaval

My whole world had just been turned upside down. Two months later, my life changed even more when three of my sisters (Pam, Karen, and Dodie) and I were moved from our home in Warsaw, Indiana to Mooseheart, a national children's home an hour west of Chicago, Illinois.

My three other siblings were on much different journeys. Don, from my dad's first marriage, had lived with his maternal grandmother in Chicago since the age of six months, and she eventually adopted him. Marg and Bob were considered too old for Mooseheart, as the age requirement was 16 or younger. Marg was 16, but Mooseheart didn't feel that she would be able to assimilate, so she stayed in Indiana and had to fend for herself. She married the first man who said he'd take care of her. My oldest brother Bob was 17 when he went into Air Force.

Many years later, we learned that we had a half-brother named Dan. We discovered that our mother had a son when she was 15, and she'd married a guy from Ohio who was 18. He went into the service, but when he came back, they realized my mother couldn't care for Dan, so his parents raised him. In 2004, we found Dan in Ohio, and he was thrilled that he had siblings. He knew we were there, but it was God who made a way for us to meet.

An Unexpected New Beginning

There were over 600 children living at Mooseheart Child City when we arrived. Because of my parents' dysfunction towards the end of their lives, I rarely had a decent meal, a nice

26

bath, or anything new. I remember to this day my trip to the "student store" after my arrival at "Child City". What an incredible feeling to have new pajamas, clean sheets, and good food! I remember the tests and visits to the doctor, the meals, but most of all shopping for clothes. I loved the feeling of having so many new things.

My sisters and I had been kept together ... but then everything changed. We were split up into different dormitories according to our ages, and so my new life began.

In the Hands of Strangers

It was lunchtime at "Baby Village", where those four years old and younger were housed. There were lots of highchairs, and they had unfamiliar food called Chicken a la King, which was served with orange Jell-O, Kool-Aid, and a sugar cookie. It was very overwhelming, because there were so many little girls staring at us with their beady little eyes.

The next feeling was panic, as the firm grip I had on my sister's hand was being pried loose. These strangers tried to make it sound so normal, but all I felt was fear and helplessness, which had become a part of adjusting to this new life.

Pam and I were just 10½ months apart when we went to where I would eventually "stay with strangers". Why were we here? So many tears that day. Mom and Dad were gone and so was my home. My familiar things had been boxed up, and I wasn't sure where anything was. My dog Statesy, a boxer who had been with me the entire four years of my life, hadn't come with. Where was Statesy? I needed her smooth satiny ears to rub and her strong body to lie down on, as a shield from all the chaos that had at times filled my former home. This situation was very difficult, because it was so unlike anything I'd previously experienced.

Resilience

That first day at "Baby Village" was mostly a blur, but I'm sure I had help getting settled. My dormmates were curious to meet me, and I was probably distracted by all the playing. However, after dinner with the new getting-ready-for-bed routine, I became very homesick for my sisters ... especially Pam.

The brand-new pajamas I had on helped a little and so did the clean comfy sheets. I loved my circus-themed headboard with the big top, clowns, and animals, and I pretended I was there. When the lights went out, I began crying and stood up in bed, so I could look out of the window. They said my sister Pam was staying at the brick building across the street, and I was very frightened without her. The housemother came in and told me to be quiet, because I'd wake the other girls. By that time, I'd worked myself up into a frenzy and was sobbing uncontrollably, but her day was over, and she was tired after caring for 14 four-year-old girls.

As I remember, the housemother was quite old, unemotional, and cold ... a product of the end of the Victorian era. Her remedy was to control and silence me. She yanked me out of bed, put me in a dark clothes closet, and locked the door. Her last words to me were, "You can come out when you've stopped crying." I fell asleep on that cold, uncomfortable closet floor that night from sheer exhaustion. I'd only been at the children's home a week, and I'd recently endured the assimilation process that every new child underwent for communal living. I learned never to let the housemother hear me cry or to do anything else that would earn punishment.

I do have a few housemothers in my heart who went above and beyond the basics. The others, although well meaning, were emotionally barren people who gave custodial care with no sense of security, individual love, value, or affection. Most of our caregivers were much older and at times just trying to survive each day.

To be honest, I've somehow blocked most of the memories of our traumatic family upheaval. It's only when I read the description of similar experiences by others that I feel the depths of my loss. Words like "alone and abandoned" would cause a lump in my throat that was hard to swallow. Who'd be my mother now? My father?

But I found no father or mother at the children's home. Most of my interactions with my housemothers and teachers, or anyone else who had to look after me, were the result of disapproval…when I did something wrong, which line I was supposed to be in, or not being in the right place at the right time. I was just a name among many, and shortly after arriving at Mooseheart, I was assigned the number L1283. This number was ironed into everything that belonged to me, and it kept my clothes separate from all the others when they went to the central laundry once a week. How sad that they didn't just use our names instead of those numbers.

Please Note: *The leadership at Mooseheart today is doing an excellent job with the children. A capable, well-screened group of family teachers works diligently to provide the love and structure each child requires to become a fully-functioning, responsible adult.*

Selah

Ted Dekker, one of my favorite authors, writes about his experiences in a boarding school after he was abandoned by his missionary parents when he was six. The sum of his life was measuring up to either avoid terrible punishment or to win favor, so he would be accepted and loved. He said it was simple, "If you say and/or do and/or believe the right things, you're golden. If you don't, you're screwed. It all depended upon you." It was just like that with God, or so I was led to believe. I was on a quest from this point on to figure out where I belonged and who was going to love me. This became the driving factor in my young life.

I see now that my entire life has been a long search for identity, value, and acceptance. I never knew or experienced the unconditional love of parents. I had to figure out how to stand out in a sea of faces. Fitting in and avoiding rejection became a full-time occupation. It's strange how resilient I was, but I had no choice. I was now in the care of strangers, so I did what I was told, adapted, and became a survivor.

It's hard to say whether this environment was better for me than living with relatives, but I'll never know. Mooseheart the "Child City" was where I was to spend my young life, until I graduated from high school. My character was strengthened by learning to live with the myriad of personalities, making me who I am today. But what was the most difficult challenge for me as a little girl? Making the connection with my heavenly Father.

How many of you started your lives in less than ideal circumstances, even in what would be considered "normal" homes? I know what that feels like, and my prayer is that as you read my life story, you will gain strength and hope. I had huge gaping holes in my soul that only my heavenly Father could fill, but I hadn't met Him yet.

"Sunshine Parents"

In Chapter 2, "Special Sundays", I'll share how God placed a special couple in my life, which impacted me on many levels. Perhaps God will remind you of those special people He brought into your life.

Chapter 2

"Special Sundays"

I shall pass thru this world but once. If, therefore, there be any kindness I can show, or any good thing I can do, let me do it now; let me not defer it, nor neglect it, for I shall not pass this way again. — *Etienne De Grellet*

SUNDAYS WERE ALWAYS SPECIAL AT THE CHILDREN'S HOME, as they were the main days that visitors came. These were times when some of the dark, empty holes in our souls, where parents and families used to reside, were temporarily filled. Oh, how we looked forward to going to the Campanile, the central meeting place for weekend guests!

In 1965, I was eight years old and had already lived at Mooseheart for over three years. I remember the day I was assigned "sunshine parents". I was told one Monday that an older couple wanted to come and visit me on Sundays! The magic had begun! With a spring in my step and joy in my heart, I tried my best to focus on my daily responsibilities. It was only Monday, and Sunday seemed like forever away to a third grader!

When Sunday finally came, I could barely make it through church, then lunch, and finally the wait for the call. The anticipation was pure torture! The phone rang, and my housemother said they'd arrived. I flew out of the door and ran two blocks to the Campanile, which was filled with families chatting and laughing. My eyes moved quickly back and forth until they stopped on an elderly couple waiting alone.

With my Sunday best on, I walked toward the Fraziers, and it was love at first sight! Most of us at Mooseheart were longing for some individual attention; and believe me … it didn't take much. I remember their warm smiles, caring eyes, graying hair, and nice-smelling perfume.

They introduced themselves to me and said, "Come, sit down, and visit with us. We want to know all about you." Well, that was all I needed to hear. I must have talked for hours; all I remember was how important I felt. They kept nodding and asking for more. Before I knew it, visiting hours were up, and I hated to see them go. They promised me they'd write and wanted to know what I wanted for Christmas!

I was delirious as I raced home and told my dorm friends about the "magical visit". It was truly a healing time for my young soul! The Fraziers remembered my birthday and other special holidays. They were always sending a card with a few quarters taped to one side.

Our times together were spent talking about how school was for me, things they were doing, and the conversation was always seasoned with lots of laughter and plenty of hugs. They brought their little toy poodle along on their visits, and I became very attached to it. With the Fraziers, I found a sense of stability and continuity. Their contact with me was one of the best things in my life. They were people I could count on.

Alone Again ...

Three years had passed, and another winter came with a vengeance. I remember waiting one Sunday for the Fraziers to come. All the possible reasons why they weren't there raced through my mind. "Where were they?", I wondered. On that cold January afternoon, I decided I'd walk down to the Campanile. I wanted to be as close as possible to the front entrance, where I could see the cars coming in. The wind was so cold on that overcast, dreary day that I decided to sit on one of the manhole covers. The hot steam seeping ever so slowly from it, took some of the chill from my 10-year-old bones.

As the hours passed, I remember the uncontrollable tears streaming down my face, stinging my icy cheeks. I knew something was wrong, I sensed it. At 5:30, I was finally forced by the evening whistle to get up and head back to my hall.

Later that evening, I received a call from Mrs. Frazier, who apologized for not coming. Mr. Frazier had suffered a heart attack on the drive out, and she was calling from the hospital. "He just went to heaven," she said. My heart sank as I tried to be brave. "I have to go now," she added, and it sounded like she was crying as she hung up. I heard from her once more, but she wasn't the same after that. I was told that Mrs. Frazier died shortly after her husband, probably from a broken heart.

I shed many tears over those losses. The pain was just too great, and it seemed like my heart had just been shut down. As sad as it was to lose such a wonderful, loving couple from my life, I'll always cherish them and how God used them to make me feel important and special.

God's Love Anchors

We all need anchors in our lives, and God's love came to me through the Fraziers. Reaching back into your memories, do you recall having God's hand on you during some of your darkest times? His love is always there for you … maybe even thru me! In Chapter 3, "Survival Academy", I'll share how I became a hardened survivor.

Chapter 3

Survival Academy

Survival: The state or fact of continuing to live or exist, especially despite difficult conditions.

By 10 years old, I believe I had stopped crying alone. I realized no one felt sorry for me, because I'd lost my family, nor would anyone comfort me. Everyone at Mooseheart, including the housemothers, were survivors too, and many of those were widows weighed down by their own sorrows.

Eventually I stopped crying altogether, because the pain of no one caring was greater than what I knew would never change. I was an orphan, a "lifer", or a child who started out in "Baby Village" and remained at Mooseheart's "Child City" until graduation. I guess you could say I was resilient, as most children are.

This place and these people were my new normal, so I slowly got with the program, started doing what I was told, and left my old life behind. My new life became an endless series of lines. We were always lining up and waiting to either eat or go to school or church.

I've no memories of ever really being alone because there were so many of us. I learned early on how many decisions were made within the "group consciousness". It was communal living, but it wasn't half bad for the most part, until I was grown and on my own.

It was difficult to make up my own mind. When I look at the few pictures I have of myself as a child from 10 years old and beyond, I either looked mad or sad. I've been told that the eyes are the windows to the soul, and they're very telling. My heart was slowly becoming hardened and rebellious. If we're not comforted and treated with value as children, then as young adults we're starved for attention, and we'll search for anything or anyone to validate us.

God has shown me more recently that I wasn't only physically orphaned, but I developed an orphan spirit, something that even people who've had both parents can succumb to. God understood my ways of coping and self-protection, and His father heart ached for me those nights I cried alone … and in the weeks, months, and years that followed.

The Dam Broke…

As I grew older, I had so many questions for God, but I wouldn't even say that I missed not having parents until I was 21. After I left the children's home, a wise counselor where I worked could see beyond my plastic smile. When I told her my life story, she said that it sounded sterile and my eyes glazed over, as if I was talking about someone else's life.

One day at lunch she came by my desk and invited me to eat with her. As she asked questions and listened, she knew I was suffering. She cleared her schedule that afternoon and brought me back to her office. I must have gone through a whole box of

Kleenex, as she asked me the right questions and I began sobbing.

It was like the dam broke, and all those years of abandonment, trauma, and having to pretend didn't work anymore. Someone cared, and as she listened, I talked and cried; it was then that my healing from abandonment began.

"Un-thawing"

As I started "un-thawing", as I called it, one of the strongest emotions was my anger towards God. He'd allowed my parents to die when He could've done something about it! But the reality is that I'll always have unanswered questions until I get to heaven.

Someone gave me the book *Disappointment with God* by the great Christian author Philip Yancey, and one of his conclusions about suffering and trauma really impacted me. He said that sometimes when a situation is irreparable, then God, in His severe mercy, comes down and intervenes. When I read that, it seemed to click, and I had something to hold onto.

God had provided me with a stable home life where my basic needs were met. I still needed healing and most of all a relationship with Him. In Psalm 23:2-3 (*NKJV*), the psalmist said that "He (God) leads me beside the still waters. He restores my soul." Like the psalmist, I also needed restoration. As Joyce Meyer (one of my favorite Christian teachers) puts it, "I may have had a rough start, but I was going to have a great ending!!!!" The truth then was and will always be, I couldn't change the events and circumstances imposed upon me, but I could choose how to respond. The mark of a person isn't just how one acts, but also how one reacts.

God sent me many counselors, and because I love to read, I found many wonderful "friends" in authors with great wisdom.

Sandra Wilson PhD, author of *Into Abba's Arms*, says our Daddy God bears no resemblance to an undependable parent, unloving spouse, unfaithful confident, a worn-out housemother (my addition), or any other person who may have disappointed, rejected, or abandoned us.

She also believes that we'll never experience life-transforming healing from abandonment, receive the ultimate acceptance we crave, or have a rock-solid sense of secure belonging, apart from an intimate, heart-to-heart relationship with Jesus Christ.

Seek His Face

I knew it was time for me to seek God's face, instead of the face of whoever had twisted His image, so I could experience His love by accepting Jesus. I also knew it was time for me to come out of survival mode and self-reliance. The Bible said I was created for love and being loved by an awesome God!

As I learned to trust Him and believe what He says about me, much healing has taken place. This journey has been hard and learning to trust God has been very difficult for me. However, I believe because of all that I've been through, He's given me enough encouragement, love and compassion for each of you as well.

Beauty Can be a Curse

I call the years between 17-21 my wild, painful, scary, and end-of-the-rope years. I had suffered so much ... how much more would I have to endure? I will reveal why I was such "A Beautiful Mess" in Chapter 4.

Chapter 4

A Beautiful Mess

As a ring of gold in a swine's snout, so is a beautiful woman who is without discretion (her lack of character mocks her beauty).

AFTER I LEFT THE CHILDREN'S HOME, I lived with my oldest sister and her family. Because I'd run away so many times to be with my boyfriend, or have some grand adventure, the leaders of Mooseheart basically washed their hands of me. I'd become incorrigible and rebellious, and they'd given up on me. My sister, who was my legal guardian, was now responsible for me. The next year and a half had weighty consequences, because I felt I knew what was best for me.

At 16, I still had much to learn about life. There were some very fun times sprinkled in with the culture shock of having lived in the absolute bubble of Mooseheart for almost 12 years. Now my sister had to sit me down and say, "I'm your sister, not your mother! You know what time you have to get to school and do your homework." The only three requirements she had for me were no drugs; don't get pregnant; and go to Beauty School, finish it, and get your license.

I was only able to do the last one, but thank God that I did, because when I turned 18, my dad's social security check stopped.

My sister then said it was time for me to branch out on my own, or basically find somewhere else to live. This began a crazy season of moving from place to place, from boyfriend to boyfriend, sometimes living alone, but mostly just moving a lot.

I started working as a hairstylist, and that atmosphere immersed me in the outside world. I had no idea how ill prepared I was for life; I was clueless about budgeting, making decisions, and living on my own, but the hardest and most painful lessons came from men.

I really enjoyed my work, and the rewards were instant approval and affirmation for great cuts and styles. I became totally obsessed with my looks and appearance. I really worked hard and played even harder.

As far back as I can remember, I was told how pretty I was. Beauty can be a curse sometimes, especially when you don't have a strong moral compass. It seemed like I could have just about any guy I wanted, but with that came significant heartache.

A Married Man

I met a salesman at a hair show in Chicago, and although I knew he was married, I started seeing him. For the next five months, I grew more and more attached to him, and I believed him when he told me of his intentions to leave his marriage.

We became intimate, which bonded me even closer to him. Then the unimaginable happened ... I found out I was pregnant! I was very naive, because I really believed that this would "seal the deal" for us. I still remember the fateful night we were parked in his car, close to his home, and the upsetting events that followed.

As I told him my news, he became agitated, extremely angry,

and he expressed his desire for me to have an abortion. My heart began to pound and then things went from bad to worse. Someone was knocking on his car window and it was his wife!

What transpired next was life shattering and left me heartbroken for seven years. He said he couldn't see me anymore and asked me to get out of his car. Did I hear him right? Surely, he didn't mean we were over. As I was walking to my car, he said to his wife, "She meant nothing to me." I was absolutely stunned … and totally devastated!!

I felt like someone had ripped my heart out and stomped on it. To this day, I honestly don't remember how I got home. Memories of him and trying to figure out how I could get him back are still very vivid. If I got rid of the baby, would he change his mind and still want me?

An Abortion

My decision to have the abortion was final. I wish I could say that I vacillated, but I didn't. I remember a girl I worked with trying to get me to change my mind. She sobbed and sobbed, but it was no use; my heart was empty and hardened. I just needed love, but I was desperate and afraid.

I remember asking a girlfriend to come with me the day of the abortion and how numb and shut down I was. After it was over, I robotically went home because I was told to rest. After a few days, I went back to work and acted like nothing had ever happened. I never saw or heard from that man again.

In hindsight, I should never have been in a relationship with a married man … or any man for that matter. At 18, one bad choice had just led to many more, which included several more abortions. It was one of the most traumatic times of my young adult life.

I already had deep wounds of abandonment from my childhood, and with this recent rejection and loss, I did what I always did … stuffed down the pain to survive. My life had become an endless quest for love and belonging.

As an adult, I now understand why leaving the children's home in rebellion at 16, with no real protection or supervision, had plunged me into an empty world of partying, alcohol, and promiscuity. In the next chapter, I'll explain how my heavenly Father pursued me, and how I was finally able to receive His unconditional love. But for now, we'll fast forward seven years to after I'd become a Christian.

A Crisis Pregnancy Clinic

I decided to go to Moody Bible Institute to pursue a counseling and communications degree. During that season, I believe God had meticulously arranged the circumstances necessary for my healing. As part of my internship, I signed up to be a lay counselor at a crisis pregnancy clinic on Michigan Avenue in Chicago. The director was a Catholic priest, and he was one of the kindest people I've ever known.

During the 1980's, there were many protests on opposing sides of the abortion issue. I remember one Saturday morning, after walking the mile from school to the clinic, I encountered a massive crowd of people carrying signs condemning abortion. They were protesting in front of the largest abortion clinic in the city of Chicago, which just happened to be two doors down from ours!

As I got closer, I couldn't believe what I was seeing…a man was holding a tiny casket with a dead fetus in it! I immediately had a panic attack, and as I made my way through the angry, judgmental crowd, I heard them screaming at the girls trying to make their way to the abortion clinic.

Some of the people were weeping for the lives of the unborn, but for the most part, they didn't care about the girls or their circumstances. At one point, someone threw a can of red paint on one of the girls and screamed, "Murderer!"

A Shameful Secret Revealed

I ran up the three flights of stairs to the safety of Father Tom's office, and I tried to compose myself. I had no idea how I could ever volunteer that morning. I'd kept this shameful secret of my abortions to myself, but I wondered how much longer I could hide the truth about what I'd done.

At the clinic, before we met with each girl or counseled them, they were required to watch a three-minute clip from the movie "The Silent Scream". The clip is from an actual abortion, and the baby, as it's dismembered in the womb, is seen screaming in excruciating pain.

When I started at the clinic, I lied and told Father Tom that I'd already seen this video. Others had warned me how graphic it was, and I just knew that I didn't want to see what I'd done to my own babies.

That day, for some reason, Father Tom had asked me to sit in the viewing room with a thirteen-year-old girl. Without her parents' knowledge, she and her boyfriend had come to Chicago from the far rural suburbs for an abortion. Our sidewalk counselors had intercepted her just in the nick of time, as they were headed straight for the doors of the abortion clinic.

As I started the video, they both sat there watching, and I still remember how sick I felt. The walls were closing in on me, and I began to shake uncontrollably. The reality and horror of what I'd done was almost too much to bear! Although I was never formally diagnosed, I'm almost certain I had PTSD.

What transpired next was God's amazing grace, healing, and forgiveness. I could barely make my way down the hall to Father Tom's office. The room was spinning, and as I sat down and looked at him, it almost seemed like he'd been expecting me. I started to cry, and I tried to talk, but all I remember was gazing into the nonjudgmental, loving eyes of Father Tom.

A Time to Heal

As I began to tell Father Tom my story, it became clear to me why I'd chosen this outreach. Somehow, I'd felt that if I could help even one girl choose life over abortion, then perhaps this would atone for my sins. I really hadn't understood or grasped the magnitude yet of why Jesus had come and what He'd died for. Father Tom told me that he'd known intuitively, but he was waiting for God's timing, so my healing could begin.

To this day, I don't know what that young girl's decision was. I've blocked out most of this experience because of the trauma, but I pray she chose life. Father Tom told me I could benefit from some counseling, and he gave me a phone number. I called the number and talked to the leader of a post-abortion support group, which I attended once a week for the remainder of the school year. The details are somewhat sketchy, but I think that's partly due to the guilt and shame I carried. Nevertheless, I'll always be grateful for that brave, honest group of women and the pain we walked through together.

A Right to Hope

I discovered that having an abortion had no age limits. One of the women in my group was in her 50's and had grown children. Ethnicity wasn't a consideration either. The group was comprised of white-collar and blue-collar workers, students, hookers, housewives, and many others. We were all part of the same club. Some say abortion was our "right" and our "choice", but most of us found out that the "simple solution" had devastating consequences.

After almost a year of struggling with the guilt and shame associated with my "choices", I decided to go back to the crisis pregnancy clinic. The difference now was that I could be there for these women from a healed place. I was no longer preoccupied with my own shame, I was there to listen and help them process the many implications of abortion. I showed compassion, and if they were open, I sometimes shared my own experiences.

One of the best tools that crisis pregnancy centers now have is ultrasound imaging. If you're reading this and considering having an abortion, please have an ultrasound first to see the baby in your womb. The post-abortion trauma statistics are staggering! My heart goes out to every woman identifying with my story, and I pray that you'll talk to someone, so you too can find help, healing, and peace.

Answers and a Family

In Chapter 5, "Final Surrender", I'll share how I finally surrendered and ran into the arms of a loving Father. For the first time, I experienced His unconditional love. Hopefully, you'll find the answers you need and surrender too!

Left
My parents: Bob and Isabel

Below
Me and my siblings. Top row: Dodie, Don, Karen. Bottom Row: Pam, Marge, Debbie. The only one missing is my brother Bob who was in the air force.

Bronze statue at entrance of Mooseheart, of James J. Davis, founder.

Mooseheart Map: an overhead view of the child city

Allegheny Hall, the first dorm I lived in. The pool was eventually redone in the shape of a red heart.

My first day at the children's home.

East Legion Hall, the dorm I lived in when I was 11.

Erie Hall, the dorm I lived in when I was 16.

Left
Marching Band baton twirlers:
Pam and Debbie

Below
Campanile at Mooseheart, where
all our visitors came.

Mooseheart House of God, where I went to church for 12 years.

Ron, Debbie and Laura

Chapter 5

Final Surrender

Surrender: Abandon oneself entirely to a powerful person, emotion, or influence.

I STILL REMEMBER THE DAY I WALKED INTO THAT SALON to interview for a job. It was 1978 and I had an abundance of confidence. I never worried about getting a job, because I had a trade, and I was very good at it. What I wasn't prepared for was the handshake I got from the manager, along with the warmest welcome reflected in her smile and eyes.

When we talked, I knew I would get the job. She liked my work, pointed to the station that would be mine, and told me to come in the next day. I was in a survival season of my life, so I started right away. I sensed immediately that there was something different about my boss Bobby, and I couldn't keep my eyes off her. I watched how she treated people, but I couldn't figure her out. I was nice to people, and I gave them good service, but I was drawn to her.

Jesus Freaks

One day after work, Bobby asked me if I'd like to come to her house for dinner. She was married and had three little kids. I was very excited to have a home-cooked meal, so I agreed. When I got to her house, I was immediately greeted by three little munchkins. The house was filled with laughter, clean laundry was piled up waiting to be folded, a dog licked my face, and finally Bobby and her husband appeared, hugged me, and said, "Ok everyone, it's time to eat."

They showed me to my place, and as we all sat down, they held hands and bowed their heads. When Bill started thanking God for the food and His blessings, I wanted to run. This was just all too familiar; I'd been taught all about God, but my upbringing had just been religion, or a list of do's and don'ts. After I left the children's home, I really wanted nothing to do with this God and all His rules, or the people who tried to make others keep them.

I thought to myself, "Oh crap, they're Jesus freaks!" The prayer ended, and we had a great dinner. I left reflecting on how nice dinner was, but I still wanted nothing to do with the church. As the weeks passed, my boss always invited me to church. She asked me almost every Saturday towards the end of the workday for almost a year. I usually had some reason why I couldn't make it, and they really were all just excuses, but it never stopped her from asking me.

An Unexpected Change of Plans

One Friday night after work, I got a call from my roommate, who was a flight attendant. She was stuck in Detroit because of a snow storm, and she wouldn't be available to go clubbing with me. I was mad of course, because everything was always about me, and this really messed up my evening.

After I hung up the phone, a wave of anxiety pulsed through me. I had no other friends to call, and as if that wasn't bad enough, we were getting a storm too. It wasn't long before my apartment lost power, and I was sitting in my living room with a few candles and a flashlight. Thoughts were racing through my head, "Just go out by yourself, you can't stay home on a Friday night, that's just unheard of! Every 21-year-old single person is out having fun, and you're stuck in here like an old person."

A Bubble Bath Encounter

I suddenly remembered that my boss had encouraged me to rest up. A huge wedding party was coming to our salon early Saturday morning, and I was going to assist her with their hair. It never bothered me before to be dead tired, running on no sleep, or dragging myself into work. However, something told me to relax and try to make the best of this unfortunate situation, so I decided to take a bubble bath and then climb into bed.

As I soaked in the tub, a sudden heaviness came over me, along with some very deep, soul-searching questions, which I'd been too busy to even contemplate, "What's your life all about? Don't you feel empty? Why don't you go to church with Bobby? You'll find answers and a family."

Somehow, I knew I was encountering the Holy Spirit. I was being drawn to Him, but I don't remember being afraid. All I knew was that for the first time in years, I was going to get a good night's sleep. I wasn't going to be hung over with the possibility of waking up next to a stranger. I was going to be invited to go with Bobby's family to church, and I could feel my heart softening and hope was flooding in.

The next morning, I was 100% ready for work. It was the first time I could remember my hands not shaking or nicking myself, as I was cutting my client's hair. The day went by fast, because we were all so focused on the bridal party. When it was time to go home, I had hardly talked to Bobby, and now she was all packed up and walking out to her car. "Oh no," I thought, "Aren't you going to ask me? You always ask me!"

A Church Invitation

At the last minute, Bobby turned around, and she told me about some Christian singing group that was going to be at her church. She thought I'd like it, and she invited me to come. Bobby almost fainted when I responded, "Yes, I'll come!" She told me to meet them at the movie theater a little before 8:00. I was thrilled and excited, but to be honest, I hadn't been up that early on a Sunday morning in years! I met them on time at an actual movie theater that their church was using. I went in with them, and I found I really did like the music as the service started. Many of the people had the same appearance as my boss; it looked like liquid love was radiating from their eyes.

Then the drama group came on stage. I watched them tell the story about a guy who had many things that the world tells you will bring happiness, success, and peace. Nevertheless, he was still walking around with a big, black empty hole in his gut. No matter what he did, he couldn't fill that hole. As I watched, the tears started streaming down my face. This was my life, and I was sure they'd prepared this little skit just for me. Bobby and her husband both put their arms around me and explained how they'd felt the same way when they first started attending this church.

My "conversion" to Christ was gradual, but after that first Sunday, I began attending church very regularly. God had a lot of work to do in my heart, because it had become so hardened. My desires started changing, and the one thing I hung onto was my pastor saying every Sunday, "God loves you." Now to the average person, such a simple declaration wouldn't seem that important; but for me, it was the start of turning my hardened, love-starved heart into something that even I barely recognized.

The two questions that drove my life were, "Who loves me and where do I belong?" I knew beyond a shadow of a doubt that I finally had a family through my church. As the months went by, I was experiencing the unconditional love of my heavenly Father! A whole new world had opened to me, and I just wanted more and more!

California Gypsy

I'd scheduled a trip to California to visit a childhood friend from the children's home. It was fun when I got there, but most of the week was filled with bars, boys, and booze. I met a guy that week who told me all the same crap I thought I wanted to hear. On top of that, my girlfriend asked me if I might consider moving to southern California. I still believe I must have a little gypsy in me, because I really didn't think about it very long before I said, "Why not?"

A few months later, this guy I barely knew flew to Chicago, and he helped me drive my little car 2,000 miles to my next home. My heavenly Father never forgot me, and He looked out for me, even though I put myself in many unbelievable situations. It wasn't long before I knew that I needed to make other living arrangements.

I was unable to use my cosmetologist's license in California, because in my haste, I'd failed to check into the state's requirements. I discovered that I'd have to go to night school for an additional 500 hours! I needed to work right away, so I answered an ad in the paper for a position, which I was very underqualified for. It was a job with a small group home for 18 developmentally handicapped adults. The eye catcher for me was the free room and board. The man and his wife who interviewed me had three other candidates apply with degrees in social work and other skills, which would've been perfect for this job. They'd considered them all, prayed, and felt like the Lord wanted them to hire me!

Final Surrender

When I tell you that the Lord really loves all of us, I mean it, because I've experienced that love. For the next year and a half, this was where I worked. I wanted to find a church there, and one of my Sunday jobs was dropping these sweet people off at their different churches. Now doesn't God have a sense of humor?!

Emmett was 61 and one of my favorite residents. He loved his church, and he asked me if I'd come with him some Sunday. When I accompanied him one Sunday, I knew right away that Calvary Chapel, Costa Mesa, was my home too! When the pastor invited those to come forward who wanted to surrender their lives to Jesus, I walked down the aisle. I was finally ready to give up my ways, and I wasn't embarrassed to let the world know it!

I became a follower of Christ that July of 1980, and I started growing in my faith. It was probably a very good thing that I was away from everything familiar back home, because I needed a fresh start in life. God knew who carried His love and could give it to a young woman with a very messed-up soul. This surrender thing was gradual, and in small doses, because I had so much survivor in me. It seemed like I had to go around the same mountain again and again and again before I decided to follow His will and His ways.

My prayer for you is that you'll learn from my many mistakes and surrender to Him as soon as possible. It's absolutely the best decision you'll ever make! I'd messed up so much with men that I took God's word to heart, and I decided to remain celibate until I got married.

Home Again

I longed for home, so in the spring of 1982, I sold my car and moved back to Illinois with about 10 boxes on a plane. I had no place to live, no car, and only the promise of a job at the salon my former boss now owned. God was way ahead of me, and when I started working, I was placed next to the most wonderful woman my age, and she became one of my best friends.

I ended up living with her and two other girls, I went back to Willow Creek Church, and I met so many new friends there. This was a very happy time in my Christian life, and God sent many opportunities my way, which healed me from the disappointments and abandonment issues I had. So much of the dissatisfaction in my life was because I hadn't connected deeply with God, the only one who could truly satisfy me.

Detour Ahead

Has your life ever taken a sudden detour? In Chapter 6, due to an unexpected trauma, I had to submit to a season of "Learning to Let God Love Me".

Chapter 6

Learning to Let God Love Me

Unconditional Love: Affection and care without limitations. It knows no bounds and is unchanging. God is Love.

IN 1985, I HAD AN EXPERIENCE THAT PRETTY MUCH rocked my world for the next year. I was 25, a student at Moody Bible Institute, and the annual missions conference was in full swing. Quite honestly, I was somewhat bored and restless, as I tried to listen to the speaker tell us about people in faraway lands who needed to know Jesus. When the session was over, there was a mass exodus from the building, as many of us headed towards ice cream and coffee shops just a few blocks away.

Struck by a Car!

In an instant, my life changed radically. I was standing on the corner with my girlfriend, waiting for the light to turn green. I wasn't paying attention, and when the light turned yellow, I began running across the busy street. I was instantly struck by a car, I flew up in the air, and then I hit the pavement on a very busy intersection of Chicago.

The next few hours, I was in and out of consciousness in the emergency room. I had a broken leg and three fractured vertebrae in my neck! When I was admitted to the hospital, I was scheduled to have a procedure known as a halo brace. In this procedure, holes are drilled on either side of the temple into the skull, and a metal brace is attached to the head for months. I know there were many people praying for me, asking God to intervene.

I had a visit the next day from the specialist, and he said they needed to wait until the swelling went down to take another x-ray. Later that night, after the x-ray had been taken, he returned to my room. With tears in his eyes, and in his thick German accent he said, "You must know someone upstairs." When he looked at the new film, something had stabilized enough in my neck, and the invasive procedure wasn't going to be necessary!

God's Amazing Ways

I was hospitalized for 22 days. I had an immobilizing neck brace, and a cast was put on my left leg that went all the way up to the top of my thigh. I was humbled many times, and I learned lessons in patience, as I waited for people to help me with my most basic needs.

I believe when we are at our weakest, God's strength comes through in amazing ways. God showed His great love towards me through caring friends and fellow classmates at Moody. I had massages, visitors from morning until evening, and professors who went out of their way to tutor me.

Guys tried to court me with wild wheelchair rides through the hospital corridors and with flowers that made my room look like a spring day. My friend Rosemary, who was with me the night of the accident, came to see me every day to help breakup the boredom. I was amazingly loved and provided for physically, emotionally, spiritually, and financially. Just days before the accident, God had prompted me to sign up for student insurance, so most of my bills were covered. The accident wasn't something God had caused, but He certainly used it for good. The compassion was overwhelming, and I could sense how God loved and cared for me through those very difficult times. I reread my journal from that timeframe, and these are a couple entries I wrote 1-2 weeks after the accident:

October 14, 1985

"Oh, this life is so unpredictable; I can't believe how suddenly things can change! I must trust God and cling to His promises because I feel so scared in this hospital. I have so much time lying here in this bed, please help me hear you God and experience Your love and nearness. Why do I have such a hard time trusting others and having them serve me? I've also noticed how hard it has been to allow myself a chance to heal and rest. I'm such an active person. I'm also a survivor. I miss the outdoors and exercise. Hospitals are such lonely places. Most people, myself included, are traumatized, drugged, anxious, and confused. Today, I've realized how blessed I am to have so many friends. All day, I've wanted to share them with all the lonely, hurting patients around me."

October 21, 1985

"Well I can't believe I'm still here flat on my back. Who could have predicted this? No more bike riding, stair climbing, walking

in the woods, or taking nice hot showers. I'm sick of people taking care of me. My thoughts are a continuous broken record. Will I be in constant pain for the rest of my life? Will I need pain medication forever? Will I have limited mobility in my neck?"

"The Fold"

After months of physical therapy, I'd recovered enough to go back to school and continue my studies in counseling and communication. I did an internship in Vermont for the summer, as a live-in housemother to six teenage girls on a 32-acre farm, about 30 miles from the Canadian border. Talk about heaven on earth for an outdoors, farm-raised woman!

We had a two-acre garden, which by the way, produced some of the most delicious tomatoes I've ever eaten! We milked cows and had 30 sheep that produced incredible wool. I watched a crusty old Vermont local shear all 30 of those sheep in less than 10 minutes! We also baked bread and had frequent visitors on the property … moose!

"The Fold" was a safe place where rebellious teens, who had gotten into trouble with the law, could find healing from the poor choices they'd made. It was a Christ-centered program, which the girls had to voluntarily choose; the alternative was going to juvenile jail. Quite honestly, it was an experience of a lifetime!

One girl at "The Fold" had been adopted from Columbia at 10 years of age. She had seen both of her parents murdered, and at 16 she was starting to rebel against her adoptive parents. When I heard her story from the head director, I began to sense that she was one of the reasons for my being there.

Agents of Love

Yes, I believe God loves each of us so much that He'll send people on special assignments as His agents of love! One night as I was leading a Friday fun time of skits and snacks, our lead housemother Annie whispered in my ear, "Would you be able to listen to this girl privately?" She knew my story and this girl had asked for me!

God used me that night to comfort her. I was very humbled, as I held her and walked her through some very intense pain and grief. The love of our heavenly Father enveloped and melted her grief-stricken heart. She made it through the entire program and was reunited with her adoptive parents.

The primary goal of the program at "The Fold" was learning about our identity in Christ. Knowing who we really are strengthens and builds up our innermost being and gives us a firm foundation upon which we can grow. I saw the beginning of transformation in these young lives, as well as my own. Look around you…God's love is waiting for you my friends. You might be surprised by who He's using right now to love you.

Enjoy His Presence

Joyce Meyer, a great Bible teacher, author, and speaker challenged me through one of her booklets, *Tell Them I Love Them*. She recommended setting aside one year to focus on every scripture about God's love and making the time to sit in His presence. She said there's a God-shaped vacuum in each of us that only God can fill.

God has been teaching me how to enjoy His presence. I can

feel His love and hear His voice. He's been WHO I'VE BEEN SEARCHING FOR ALL MY LIFE!!! When I come to Him just as a little child and crawl up into His lap, and I stop trying to do life in my own strength, He meets me.

For those of you who aren't quite sure, take some time to let God reveal Himself to you. He'll never let you down. His love will heal you and fill you up to overflowing, so you'll have enough love to share with those around you!

Plunged into Grief

Chapter 7 is very painful. "I'll Hold You in Heaven" is my tribute to Melissa Joy.

Chapter 7

I'll Hold You in Heaven

We never got a chance to know you, but we shall someday.

At thirty, I married a wonderful man. We were best friends who loved God and His people. After a few years together, I became pregnant with our first child. It was a happy time, but our church family was comprised of mostly young single adults and married couples with no children, so a few other women and I were pioneering the pregnancy phase.

Stillbirth

I was close to my due date and very uncomfortable. As I lay in bed that night, I felt my child thrashing around inside of me. Something was very wrong, so I called my doctor, and he said to come in the next morning for an ultrasound.

The ultrasound detected no heartbeat. A few days later, labor was induced, and my firstborn daughter Melissa Joy was born. Because she hadn't taken a breath of life, she was considered stillborn. The umbilical cord had ruptured, and her oxygen supply had been cut off. She was fully formed and beautiful, with lots of brown hair, my button nose, and she had the appearance of just being asleep.

What was supposed to be one of the happiest times for a couple, turned into a nightmare. My husband and I were plunged into grief. The intense feelings of anxiety and despair almost destroyed us both. No one wants to lose anyone they love, but a child's death seems especially cruel. The nursery was almost set up, and the baby showers had been thrown. Everything was ready, but there was no baby to bring home … and we never had the opportunity to be a family.

Goodbye to Our Baby Girl

I'll never forget how defeated I felt, when I left the hospital with no prize for all my hard labor. I remember seeing the paperwork in my room. Our daughter had been taken to the morgue, and then the funeral home would be picking her up.

The funeral was attended by numerous people. I was numb and drugged, so my recollection of that day is sketchy. I remember it was a cold, damp, overcast, January day in Chicago. When they put the little white casket in the back of that huge hearse, I remember sitting in the car behind it wanting to scream and wail until the world stopped.

But everything continued as usual, and everyone just went about their everyday activities, while we said goodbye to our baby girl. That night after the people left, all I wanted to do was sleep to escape the pain … my arms ached to hold Melissa one more time.

At the funeral home, before the people came, we had our final moments with Melissa. My husband and I committed each one of her tiny details to memory. She was dressed in a pink outfit with a sweet frilly bonnet, and she was wrapped in a baby blanket.

My wonderfully kind husband had gone to a baby store to find that bonnet, which was to cover the soft spot where her skull hadn't closed yet. A salesperson at the store asked if this was his first, and he shared the sad news that this bonnet would be buried on our precious daughter's head.

Intense Grief

I distinctly remember listening to Mike Kellogg's program "Music Through the Night" on Moody Radio during the difficult delivery process. His voice was incredibly soothing as he quoted scripture and played some of the best worship music. I listened to him for many months after Melissa's death, when I struggled with insomnia. He was truly a blessing to me during a very traumatic time.

One thing I know for sure is how intense grief can be. The shock of what I'd just gone through made me feel almost crazy. My milk had just started coming in, and my doctor told me to stand in the shower to relieve the pressure. I looked forward to that great escape where grief couldn't find me ... and then I finally fell asleep.

Three weeks after Melissa died, our church family surprised Ron and I with a paid trip to California. It was a very generous gift, and many had given sacrificially, so we could get a little rest and relaxation. When we arrived, I wasn't prepared for the intense pain I was experiencing.

We tried to go to Disneyland, but that only lasted a couple hours. I was overwhelmed by all the moms with strollers, and it seemed like all the baby girls had bonnets on to shade them from the California sun. My husband Ron was very patient with me that week because all I wanted to do was sit in our hotel room.

Ron would gently encourage me to take a drive with him, and he would surprise me with some of the most beautiful spots in southern California. The healing had begun, and we fell in love with La Jolla, which is an exceptionally breathtaking place. We sat and gazed upon the beautiful Pacific Ocean for hours, and we watched the sea lions bark and play. We marveled at the scope and exquisiteness of God's creation ... and it was good!

Don't Wound the Wounded

Some well-meaning people in the coming weeks and months following Melissa's death wounded us even more with their insensitivity. Most people aren't equipped to deal with the suffering and pain of others. Some people genuinely wanted to console us, but they really didn't know what to say or do. Somehow, I believe they wanted to hurry us through our grief, because I think it made them uncomfortable.

When tragedy and suffering happen, people feel like they must have answers or reasons; they really want to rescue us from that pain. I've never heard so many trite clichés or received so much unsolicited advice. It got to the point that I felt unprotected and defenseless, because I had no idea what people were going to say next. I began isolating myself, since there weren't many I felt safe with.

A Season of Mourning

If only people knew that those who are grieving simply need others to be there with and for them. Just talking about who we lost really helps; please say their name and something you remember about them. The people who helped my husband and I the most were those who came over to do whatever; they prepared a meal, cleaned our home, paid our bills, and a few just sat with us and listened, as we wept and retold the experience over and over.

Eventually our season of mourning came to an end. All these years later, as I write this chapter, my prayer is that in reading this, you'll either become a helper to someone in grief, or you'll better understand the grieving process when a loved one passes.

For the griever, I have several websites where you can get help listed at the end of this book. I'd start with your family and circle of friends, asking them to just listen. For the helper, I have several books and sites for you too. I'm very passionate about this universal occurrence, which none of us can escape. It's essential that others become helpers and healers when those monster-sized waves crash unexpectedly after a loss.

Working Through Grief

My greatest healing came when I cried, spoke to God, talked with others, walked, worshipped, slept, and when I was eventually used to help others. I don't believe that "time heals all wounds". I've met some very bitter, broken people, with profuse unforgiveness in their souls. They'd talk about their losses, as if they'd just occurred the previous day.

Grief takes work, but it's worth the effort, instead of pretending, withholding the tears, stuffing those feelings down, or staying medicated. My prayer is that after reading my story, you might consider exploring how you've helped or hurt others in the past either by your ignorance or words. While we're still living on this planet, it's a reality we must all face. We are left with grief when people we love die. Grief, by definition, is a deep emotional response to a great loss; the loss of someone we love and value who is no longer in our lives.

May you know and experience, *"The Father of compassion and the God of all comfort, who comforts us in all our troubles, so we can comfort those in any trouble with the comfort we ourselves receive from God."* (2 Cor 1:3-4)

Tears of Joy and Thankfulness

After I lost Melissa Joy, I wanted to get pregnant again right away. Each month would come and go, and I'd take a pregnancy test without success. Approximately 15 months later, we finally did conceive. The nine-month gestation period seemed like nine years, because of all the anxiety of wanting our baby to be born healthy and alive.

We chose a home birth with our close friends there cheering me on. On February 3, 1992, Ron and I became the proud parents of Laura Michelle. When I heard her first cry, and the doctor put her on my chest, all I remember was Ron holding us both very close. There were many tears of joy and thankfulness, as I gazed into Laura's eyes. I can't describe the relief we felt, as we studied her precious little fingers and toes. It was God's wisdom and His perfect timing to bless us with another child.

Ron and I thoroughly enjoyed parenthood, and we did try to have more children. Looking back though, I think it was a half-hearted effort, because of the lingering fear of losing another child.

Three Significant Moves

After a vacation in Florida, when Laura was 18 months old, we decided to move to Sarasota to be closer to Ron's parents. We spent almost 10 years there, and we made some wonderful friends, but the restlessness had begun to grow. We went to an incredible worship conference in Kansas City, Missouri. Within days of returning home, we put our house in Florida on the market, and it sold in 12 hours! Seven weeks later, our adventure began, as we started the School of Prayer at the International House of Prayer (IHOP) in Kansas City.

So many incredible memories and lots of growth later, I longed to be back in Illinois. I wanted to be closer to my siblings, and I wanted Laura to know her family. That's when we made another move back to the Chicago suburbs.

"There's Hope for Any Marriage"

Have you ever wanted to run away from your marriage? After 19 years together, I decided to separate from my husband. In Chapter 8, "I Do Again", we'll look at how God restores broken marriages. Sometimes the answer isn't who we run from, but Who we must run to in our times of need.

Chapter 8

"I Do Again"

Covenant: An agreement which brings about a relationship of commitment between God and His people.

BE CAREFUL WHEN YOU SAY YOU'LL NEVER DO SOMETHING ... because that may be the very thing you end up doing!

I was married for almost 19 years when I decided to separate from my husband Ron. Looking back, I understand some of the reasons, but mostly I was lonely. I had no direction or purpose in my life, my daughter had entered the teen years and wanted to be with her friends all the time, and I felt like no one needed me.

I now know that I needed a revelation of how much I was loved by my heavenly Father, because I'd been desperate to feel loved by my husband. There was a lot brewing beneath the surface of our marriage, which I learned about years later. The most outstanding problems were our lack of emotional intimacy and financial struggles. I remember waking up one morning and realizing that I just couldn't live like this anymore. I was choosing to give up.

The next thing I did was look for a job. I'm a hairstylist, so I was able to find a job to support myself, and then I began looking for an apartment. My husband and I rarely fought, so when I told him I was moving out, it was a very miserable day. By this time, I was numb, my heart had shut down, and I really didn't want to seek guidance.

I found a cute little place in an old Victorian house, and the transition into my new life seemed easy, at least on my end. I had feelings of freedom and confidence, but there was also a sense of failure and a fear of being on my own.

Mid-Life Crisis

I didn't stop to think about how my decisions were affecting my daughter Laura, because I was only thinking about myself. Years later, I was finally able to ask forgiveness for all the pain I had caused her and my husband, and I was also able to forgive myself. I still can't believe I was separated for five years and divorced for two years.

During the separation period, I attempted to divorce my husband twice, and we tried counseling in between. Something wouldn't let me go through with the divorce, so we were stuck in limbo. At the same time, I left the church we'd been attending. Years later, I realized I had some very deep wounds. I really didn't know God as my Father or what it meant to be a follower of Christ. I was lost and had relapsed into survivor mode, again.

I didn't pray or read my Bible. I had no one in my life who cared about me or even challenged my decisions. My two sisters were as helpful as they could be, but I was in a crisis of my own making. They watched from the sidelines and listened to the drama when they could. My sisters both loved my husband Ron, so it was difficult for them to just listen to my side of the story. Most of the women I'd befriended didn't know how to embrace or love me, while still holding true to their convictions that God hated divorce.

I had numerous experiences where my heart was crushed by the judgments or public disapprovals of me, which pushed me further away from God, the church, or healing. The specifics of this time escape me, due to my shame and self-loathing. I also started doing two things, which had both been long gone from my life ... drinking and smoking!!

During that season, I believe I was in what the world would describe as a "mid-life crisis". I don't think I even understood what marriage was about. Love to me meant, "I love you, do you love me?" My principal foundation was built upon very shaky ground. When the trials of life came, I wanted to run to something that was much easier and more fun.

That period between 2005-2012 was heart wrenching, but my husband Ron was faithful, and he never took off his wedding band. On various special occasions, he'd leave a sweet card on my car windshield. I thought it was nice, but it didn't change my hardened heart.

Betrayed Again

Although I never once felt good about it, I ended up going through with the divorce. The strangest part about all of it was that my husband and I remained on reasonably good terms. We'd get together for our daughter's school events, and sometimes for family gatherings, but I was still moving on. I'd developed a relationship with someone else, thinking that he'd have new answers for my old brokenness.

He showered me with attention and helped me financially. There was even the promise of a ring and stability. All I know is that I was being filled up emotionally. I was like a drug addict needing my regular fix, and I lived for his phone calls. After he called, my emotional love tank overflowed.

He'd recently finalized his divorce, so the future seemed bright, but something didn't feel right. There was a weird gnawing deep inside me that I just couldn't put my finger on. It was as if the Holy Spirit wasn't going to allow any further damage in my life. One night, when I was already in bed, He prompted me to get up and drive to this man's house.

When I arrived, I had this premonition that I was going to discover something very distressing. I had his garage door opener, and as I went in, I knew another woman was there. I called out his name, and I could tell he was very intoxicated by the way he ambled down the stairs. When he came outside, I asked him why he'd cancelled our dinner plans. There was no getting through to him in that state, so I decided to go back inside and face whatever was upstairs.

When I turned the corner to the bedroom, there was a woman passed out in his bed. I was so devastated that I turned and flew down those stairs! I believe I called my sister that night and a few other friends, but I was inconsolable. Once again, I'd been betrayed. I really thought he cared about me and wanted us to have a future together.

The next few weeks and months were a blur. I broke things off, but I found myself in a place of mourning and almost despair, because I'd grown so accustomed to his attention. If it wasn't for God's intervention, I'm not sure where I'd be today. Through a Christian friend, I found a group of believers that met on Friday nights. I decided to accompany her, and it felt good to be around the body of Christ again.

Rest for My Soul

Because I had fallen and broken my wrist a few weeks earlier, I could no longer work as a hairstylist, and my world began unraveling very quickly. I can now see how God's hand had provided for me in ways too numerous to recount.

One of the kindest things that God did for me was to guide me to a safe place where I could find rest for my soul. The leaders of the Friday night gathering I'd been attending were very loving and invited me into their home. I stayed with them for nine months, and I tried to do things to help them around their house. To this day, I don't know if they really understood how bad my situation was emotionally and spiritually.

I'm normally an extrovert, but during this season, I found myself shying away from others … especially on Sundays. People would come to the house for church, stay for lunch, and sometimes it would last for three to four hours. It was there that I met the woman who God has used to love me in some very deep ways.

When I first met Jill, I was overwhelmed by how full of life she was. I felt like a shell of a person, but as I sat and talked with her, God showered me with kindness. She spoke encouraging words to me that literally left me sobbing. Doesn't she know what I've done? If she did … it didn't seem to matter to her.

By the end of that meeting, she put her arms around me and asked if I'd like to stay with her. I didn't even know her, but I was drawn to her. She was a traveling nurse, divorced, and she had two teenagers. She and I were able to work out a plan that would be a win-win situation.

In an incredibly selfless act, Jill's son Adam gave me his room for nine months and slept on the couch. Jill also decorated his room for me in such a lovely way! Why were they doing all this for me? In retrospect, I was a prodigal daughter that God had gone after. I was a lamb that had lost its way, and God had used Jill to help restore me. The time that I spent there was like salve to my soul.

Jill's kids were incredible, and we had many fun times together. I began working again on a limited basis and that was good. Jill sat me down one evening to talk, because she knew I was struggling with my bills. She allowed me to use her credit card, and she said that I could pay her back when I was in a better place! Who does this?! It was so generous that I could hardly speak!

I was now able to work with less stress and know that my bills would be paid. After nine months, it was time for me to give Adam his room back. I moved into a new season that really stretched me, but in hindsight, it was the perfect decision.

A Daily Battle

I decided to take the position as a companion to an elderly woman. As part of my compensation, I'd receive free room and board. When I met her, I realized what a challenge this was going to be. She was a survivor, just like I was, and she didn't need help, or so she thought.

It was a daily battle, and sometimes I just wanted to walk out, but something wouldn't let me. I had been slowly reading my Bible again, and I was trying to listen to the still small voice of God. He wanted me to care for her because He loved her, even if she had nothing to give in return! Isn't that what I'd been given?

I was stunned by what felt like an impossible task, because

she was so unlovable! All I saw were her prickles and barbs, but God wanted me to love her with His love. Every day, I'd spend time with my heavenly Father, and then I could cheerfully greet her and serve her the best I knew how.

I tried to get her to do different things, but her comfort zone was one small room in her big, beautiful home. She had a gorgeous backyard with mature oak trees and birdfeeders, so one day I asked her if she wanted to sit outside, and she reluctantly agreed.

I'll never forget the moment when she let go of her walker and grabbed my arm. She was terrified, as I guided her down the three steps to her patio. When we made it, I saw relief in her eyes, but I also saw a woman who very much needed someone, and her heart began to soften.

My days were long, but I had my daily routine with big chunks of free time. Part of my job description was to cook for her, and she was quite picky. Eventually, I ended up buying TV dinners and presenting them as her evening meal. I must admit I took the complements, even though it was really Marie Callender's coming through for me.

God accomplished much in my heart during this season. My ex-husband Ron and daughter Laura became regular visitors to Nancy's house, and she welcomed them, as she and I became closer. I lived with her for a year and three months, and it was only by God's grace that I was able to do so. Who would've thought that I'd be watching Jeopardy and Wheel of Fortune!!!

I started longing for my own space again, and I knew it was time for me to start looking. I still wanted to work for her, but not stay overnight. I had no bills, so I'd saved for rent. I found a cute little studio on the historic Woodstock square. Nancy's family hated to see me move, but I was still allowed to take care of their mom, for which I was grateful. My ex-husband Ron was also living in Woodstock, so we'd meet up for a meal every now and then.

There's Hope for Any Marriage

One day as I was driving, I heard the most amazing woman being interviewed on Moody Radio. She was telling her story, which was incredibly like mine! She'd been separated for five years and divorced for two years. She was angered by betrayal, full of disappointment, and she was wrestling with God. As I drove and listened, I remember not paying that much attention at first, until I heard her say, "There's hope for any marriage."

I perked up and increased the volume, so I could hear every word. I think it was an hour-long interview. There was so much transparency and vulnerability that I had to pull over towards the end, because I was sobbing so hard. I fumbled to find a pen and paper, so I could write down the name of her book. At the same time, I humbly prayed and asked God if He could restore my marriage.

For the first time in seven years, I felt hope flooding my being and my hardened heart melting. I quickly drove to the Christian bookstore, purchased the book, and read it in one day. I believe God was preparing and opening my heart for reconciliation.

I asked God what I was to do, and He whispered in that still small voice, "Go back to your husband and daughter to give, not to get. Write them a letter and tell them you're sorry for the part you played in the breakdown of your family. Let Me do the rest!"

He Never Promised It Would be Easy

By that time, Ron had pretty much given up on anything ever changing between us. Our daughter Laura was involved with friends and school, while trying to deal with her mom and dad's new normal.

I cried as I wrote down all the things I'd done. The selfishness of my choices flooded the pages, as I asked for forgiveness. One day I asked them both to sit down and listen, as I read them those pages. All I can say is they weren't ready to jump on that bandwagon or believe a word I said!

That was one of my biggest fears ... I would open my heart, but Ron and Laura wouldn't be able to trust me again. God continued to draw my attention with daily reminders about how I'd genuinely desired to surrender to Him and how I must follow where He was leading. I listened when He told me that He never promised it would be easy.

One of my journal entries at that time was about a reality, which I really needed to comprehend:

> *This reconciliation wasn't about me, but it was God's desire for my life and the lives of my family. This was about God getting the glory, not me. I presumed that once I was willing to believe God for the restoration of my marriage, then He would quickly come through with the results...and in my timing, of course. It was much slower than I thought it would be, but looking back, I was on God's timetable.*

I Do Again

Ron and I began dating and rekindled our romance. We decided that the three of us should look for a new home, and we found a beauty right on a lake near family and friends. We had our first Christmas there, and as we all opened our gifts, I received a proposal and a ring that was more than I ever could have imagined!

It was such a miracle and an incredibly healing time for our family! The year 2012 began a new chapter together, which was filled with having friends and family over for visits.

On September 24, 2013, we got remarried in our beautiful backyard with our daughter Laura singing a song she wrote. There were no dry eyes, as our guests watched us read our vows and tell a few funny stories. We celebrated late into the night and then sent people on their way ... knowing that they'd just witnessed a miracle!

The God of Hope

Back in 2005, if you'd asked me if I thought that my marriage could ever be reconciled, my answer would have been a resounding, "NO!" I felt like our relationship was hopeless. I never dreamt that our marriage could be restored to something beyond what we'd dared to ask or hope for. God did it ... He's bigger than our problems. He's the God of hope!

As I finish up this chapter, I wondered why it had taken me so long to write it. I believe the reasons were shame and the fear of man. God reminded me in His Word, *"Therefore, there is now no condemnation for those who are in Christ Jesus."* (Romans 8:1)

It's the truth that sets us free, and I finally decided that I wanted to come out of the shadows to share this amazing journey with others. My intent in being honest and sharing our story was so that I could convey how amazing God is. I wanted to share how human we are and what an amazing miracle transpired when we just said yes to His plan.

I believe that most people don't really understand what marriage is about ... I know I didn't. God said that we were first created to be in relationship with Him. In Luke 10:27, we're instructed to, *"Love the Lord your God with all your heart and with all your soul and with all your strength and with all your mind; and, love your neighbor as yourself."*

Most of us were broken coming into relationships, longing to be filled, but not knowing God or putting Him first. Secondly, we didn't really love ourselves, which makes it difficult to love your spouse when you're empty. Most of us didn't have good role models to show us the way, but that's ok, because it's God who redeems marriages.

Here's some additional wisdom my husband and I received ... just because we're back together and working on our marriage doesn't automatically mean that things are always going to be perfect. It takes time for people to heal. I really believe that when I decided to come back to our marriage, I drew a line in the sand, I made a covenant with my husband, and there was no escape clause. Even though it's still hard at times, I keep going, because I truly believe it's what God wants!

May your hearts be moved to invite God in, so that you may also live a renewed and more joyous marriage. I'm rooting for you!!

A Powerful Gift

Maybe you haven't had as many disappointments and hurts as I have, but we all have people in our lives who have wronged us. In Chapter 9, we'll look at why you should "Do Yourself a Favor and Forgive". Sometimes it's incredibly difficult, but I believe that forgiveness is one of the most important things we can do!

Chapter 9

Do Yourself a Favor and Forgive

Then Peter came to Him and said, "Lord, how often shall my brother sin against me, and I forgive him? Up to seven times?"
Jesus said to him, "I do not say to you, up to seven times, but up to seventy times seven." (Matthew 18:21-23, NKJV)

FORGIVENESS ISN'T ALWAYS EASY! At times, forgiving the person who wounded you seems more painful than the wound itself, but without forgiveness, there's no peace or healing!

I believe this is one of the most important chapters in my book. I want to say up front that I don't have all the answers. All I really have to offer is my own experience, strength, and hope. Many good books have been written on the topic of forgiveness; so please, consider me a fellow struggler like yourself.

Jesus must have known we'd say and do things that would require forgiveness. My faith has taught me that we're to forgive each person who has wronged us up to seventy times seven! With all my heart, I believe forgiveness is one of the most powerful gifts we can give, not only to ourselves, but to those who have wronged us.

Choosing to Forgive

I'd like to share two very difficult situations that angered me and caused great pain. As a result, I had to willingly choose to forgive the persons involved.

The first person I had to forgive was one of the leaders at the children's home where I grew up. Years after I left, I discovered that he'd obtained some very intimate letters I'd written to my boyfriend, and he shared them with many of the staff. This leader was also one of the staff that branded me a "boy-crazy troublemaker".

I know that God wanted me to have the liberty to visit my childhood home free of guilt, shame, or condemnation. Therefore, I had to willingly choose to forgive this man. By no means was this easy, but it was very freeing!

The next time I had to choose forgiveness was after we lost our firstborn, Melissa. It was a spring morning and all the snow had melted at her gravesite. As I approached the headstone, I'd expected to see green grass where the ground had been disrupted, but it was early spring, and the grass wasn't actively growing yet. It had only been about two months since Melissa's death, and my emotions were still very raw.

At church that morning, as I was singing worship songs to God, the tears started flowing, accompanied by some intense grieving. I made it to the end of the service, and as my husband and I were in the foyer, we overheard two young adults judging my inability to "get over it and move on". Their comments were very insensitive and heartless. Somewhere in that season, with God's encouragement, I forgave them.

I did write a note to one of the guys months later about his lack of compassion. Years later, after he'd married, he sent me the kindest letter. He now had a daughter of his own and had gained understanding.

Most people don't intentionally mean to harm us. They do so just because they're human, and they don't think about the consequences of their words and/or actions.

Basics of Forgiveness

I'd like to share with you what I believe forgiveness is in laymen's terms. There are three basic steps in the process of forgiveness, which are the same for everyone:

1. We rediscover the humanity of the person who hurt us.
2. We surrender our right to get even.
3. We change our mind about the person we forgave.

Whenever I need to forgive someone, I find that these three steps are very helpful. When these basics have been achieved, you have entered the healing process.

Forgiveness is the Better Way

Like the title of this chapter, the first reason we need to forgive is … to do ourselves a favor. Forgiveness releases our own pain, and the outflow of that decision can heal the pain of others. I once read the following story, which is just one example of why forgiveness is the better way:

There was a man of seventy who said he was cheated out of a promised retirement bonus fifteen years ago. He knew for sure who was responsible; it was the new vice-president in charge of personnel.

Everyone who spent more than fifteen minutes with this man, heard his story. Every taxi driver who drove him for more than two miles, the postman, and the woman at the checkout counter all knew his story, which he spewed upon whoever would listen.

His rage became his very being. He is his bitterness. He breathes it, sleeps with it, and will probably die with it. The poison of bitterness has splattered his organs, and he now has a bleeding ulcer in the lining of his once healthy stomach. But he's waited too long; if he forgave now, he'd no longer know who he was. His anger, hatred, and bitterness are now a part of his being.

He could still choose to forgive, and maybe he will, but his prolonged postponements have made forgiveness dreadfully hard. It's so sad that many people don't want to risk forgiving too quickly, so they wait, and they wait, and they wait. My encouragement to you is to have forgiveness in your character, so at the prompting of the Holy Spirit, you'll be ready and willing to forgive. Don't let it fester and turn back on you!

Why Don't People Forgive?

The reason I've chosen to forgive all those who have hurt me is because I'm a forgiven person, which goes back to my faith. I'm an imperfect person, I'm thankful when others forgive me, but mostly I'm grateful that I've been forgiven by God.

Lewis Smedes, the author of *The Art of Forgiving*, says that we forgive when we want to heal ourselves from the hangover of a wounded past. So, you might ask "Why don't people forgive?" Some people have a primitive need to protect their pride, some don't want to appear weak, while others have moral instincts for justice.

I've heard people say that if they forgive so and so, then they're just inviting them to stab them in the back again. Or are we just minimizing what they did and implying that what happened wasn't all that bad? Some people feel that if they forgive someone who wronged them, or someone they love, then they're giving them a pass from the demands of justice.

By nature, I'm a simple person and very child-like. I've embraced forgiveness in a very practiced way for the last 10 years. Before then, I thought I was a forgiver, but God revealed some hidden places in my heart that weren't so forgiving.

Having been on both sides of it, I'll take being a forgiver any day. It makes me feel so free and at peace. Forgiving myself has been done in stages, and for some of the choices I've made, it has been difficult. It helps when I ask myself, "If I had to choose to do the same thing now, with who I am, and what I know … would I?" My answer is usually, "No." As a believer in Jesus, I demonstrate compassion to myself when I choose to learn from my mistakes and not live in regret.

Why You Should Forgive

I've read in various places, that hospitals and mental institutions would empty out if people could forgive. Hurting people in prison would have peace if they could forgive themselves. I could go on and on with significant reasons why it's important to forgive. I believe it's the only way to heal the wounds of the past that we cannot change or forget. As you contemplate why you should forgive, consider these quotes taken from *The Art of Forgiving* by Lewis Smedes:

- We do our forgiving alone inside our hearts and minds; what happens to the people we forgive depends on them.
- The first person to benefit from forgiving is the one who does it.
- We forgive people only for what they do, never for what they are.
- Forgiving is a journey; the deeper the wound, the longer the journey.
- Waiting for someone to say they are sorry before we forgive is to surrender our future to the person who wronged us.
- Forgiving is not a way to avoid pain but to heal pain.
- Forgiving is essential; talking about it is optional.
- When we forgive, we set a prisoner free and discover that the prisoner we set free is us.

It's Your Choice ... Justice or Grace

Satan is a legalist, and when you choose justice, you've stepped into his realm, a life bound by the legal restraints of this world. Legalism offers no forgiveness, restitution at best, and you become trapped in the justice system, until you step up into grace.

When you chose grace, you've entered God's realm. Grace gives you the freedom to move into a place of forgiveness, followed by restoration, and the opportunity for relationship. It's relationship that opens the door to healing

John Arnott has an excellent booklet titled What Christians Should Know About ... the Importance of Forgiveness, in which he fully explains the difference between justice and grace. He recommends giving people a gift they don't deserve … forgiveness. The act of forgiving frees you and releases them!

Jesus gave a very strong warning about unforgiveness in Matthew 6:15, *"But if you do not forgive others their sins, your Father will not forgive your sins."*

Please don't wait any longer … FORGIVE!

Who He Says I Am

Most of us weren't properly prepared to have a successful life. One of the biggest blessings is revealed in Chapter 10 where it's determined, "Who are You … Really?"

Chapter 10

Who Are You ... Really?

"When your identity is found in Christ, your identity never changes. You're always a child of God." — Tim Tebow

I'VE BEEN SEARCHING FOR THE ANSWER to that question my entire life! As you've already read, I lived my young adult life as a "fool". My two biggest questions were, "Where do I belong and who will love me?"

Before I knew who I really was ... I had a very shaky foundation built upon shifting sand. In Matthew 7:24-27 (*TLB*), Jesus said, *"All who listen to my instructions and follow them are wise, like a man who builds his house on solid rock. Though the rain comes in torrents, and the floods rise, and storm winds beat against his house, it won't collapse, for it is built on rock. But those who hear my instructions and ignore them are foolish, like a man who builds his house on sand. For when the rains and floods come, and storm winds beat against his house, it will fall with a mighty crash."*

In the past, my identity was based upon what I did; my value was derived from who said they loved me; and my belonging was generally connected to a man and his life. I really was just tossed around from place to place. I finally realized, with God's help, that I was looking for love and acceptance in all the wrong places.

We all have a deep need to belong, which even carries over into the church. We are sons and daughters of the King, and it's important we recognize that, or even the church can mess us up with performance-based acceptance, being in with the right crowd, or serving to find our worth and belonging. There's a big difference between being a child of God, an heir of the Kingdom, and trying to work our way into heaven.

"When God our Savior revealed his kindness and love, He saved us, not because of the righteous things we had done, but because of His mercy." (Titus 3:4-5, *NLT*)

Who God Says We Are

The last seven months, I've been participating in an online mentoring group led by Patricia King, one of my favorite "spiritual mothers". She says that your "true" identity isn't what others say about you … it's what God says about you! In the Bible, God says:

- We are His beloved children. (John 1:12)
- We are the righteousness of God. (2 Corinthians 5:21)
- We are fellow heirs with Jesus. (Galatians 4:7, Romans 8:16-17)
- We are the light of the world. (Matthew 5:14)
- We are the temple of God. (2 Corinthians 6:16)
- We are the object of His love and affection. (John 3:16)
- We are the apple of His eye. (Psalm 17:8)
- We are forgiven, clean, and pure. (1 John 1:9)
- We are a recipient of all His promises. (2 Peter 1:4)
- We are overcomers. (Revelation 12:11)

And on and on it goes!

Patricia King continues her teaching with how valuable we are to God. We're unique and irreplaceable. Amongst the billions of people in the world, no two humans ever have the same fingerprints, retinal patterns, or genetic makeup...they simply aren't alike!

Jesus valued us so much that He paid the ultimate price by shedding His blood and giving His life. If we understood our value, we'd treat ourselves differently. If we understood the value of others, we'd treat them accordingly. We become what we value!

I now know how valuable I am, and my worth isn't determined by my childhood, what others have spoken over me, or my performance. Honestly, this has been one of the most healing, freeing, peace-producing revelations I've ever received!

"Identity Robbers"

"The thief does not come except to steal, and to kill, and to destroy. I have come that they may have life, and that they may have it more abundantly." (John 10:10, NKJV)

Early in my walk as a believer, I discovered that Satan is our enemy, whose primary goal is to destroy the children of God. He would like to take as many people to hell with him as possible, because he knows that pierces the heart of God. With his lies, he tries to blind and mislead Christians, so they don't know who they are or what their true inheritance is.

"From the very beginning he (Satan) was a murderer and has never been on the side of truth because there is no truth in him. When he tells a lie, he is only doing what is natural to him, because he is a liar and the father of all lies." (John 8:44, GNT)

Satan is very adept and cunning. He'll throw stumbling blocks in the paths of unsuspecting Christians to create feelings of self-doubt or unworthiness. "Identity robbers" are just some of the tools in Satan's arsenal, used as diversions to derail God's children, as he plays upon their fragile human emotions. The following "identity robbers" were all present in my life:

- Accusation
- Comparison
- Competition
- Condemnation

- Jealousy
- Lies
- Shame
- Soul-wounding

How then do we fight such a vicious and determined enemy? In Ephesians 6:11-18 (*TPT*), we're instructed to,

Put on God's complete set of armor provided for us, so that you will be protected as you fight against the evil strategies of the accuser! Your hand-to-hand combat is not with human beings, but with the highest principalities and authorities operating in rebellion under the heavenly realms. For they are a powerful class of demon-gods and evil spirits that hold this dark world in bondage. Because of this, you must wear all the armor that God provides so you're protected as you confront the slanderer, for you are destined for all things and will rise victorious.

Put on truth as a belt to strengthen you to stand in triumph. Put on holiness as the protective armor that covers your heart. Stand on your feet alert, then you'll always be ready to share the blessings of peace.

In every battle, take faith as your wrap around shield, for it is able to extinguish the blazing arrows coming at you from the

*Evil One! Embrace the power of salvation's full deliverance, like
a helmet to protect your thoughts from lies. And take the mighty
razor-sharp Spirit-sword of the spoken Word of God.*

As I replaced Satan's lies with the truth (who God says I am),
my life became abundantly filled with the fruit of the Spirit (love,
joy, peace, patience, kindness, goodness, faithfulness, gentleness,
and self-control). My life's now free from condemnation, guilt,
and shame. I'm in right standing with God, my heavenly Father,
who created me before time began to be in relationship with
Him, so I'd receive His unconditional love.

Our Omniscient God

In Luke 12:6-8, we see how God loves and values His creation, but also how intimately acquainted He is with each one of
us, *"Are not five sparrows sold for two pennies? Yet not one of them
is forgotten by God. Indeed, the very hairs of your head are all num-
bered. Don't be afraid; you are worth more than many sparrows."*
One of my favorite scriptures is Psalm 139. I'd like to share
several incredible passages from this Psalm that reveal His numerous thoughts about us!

*You have searched me, LORD, and you know me. You know when
I sit and when I rise; you perceive my thoughts from afar. You
discern my going out and my lying down; you are familiar with
all my ways. Before a word is on my tongue you, LORD, know it
completely. You hem me in behind and before, and you lay your
hand upon me. Such knowledge is too wonderful for me, too lofty
for me to attain." (Psalm 139:1-6)*

"How precious to me are your thoughts, God! How vast is the sum of them! Were I to count them, they would outnumber the grains of sand - when I awake, I am still with you." (Psalm 139:17-19)

"I praise you because I am fearfully and wonderfully made; your works are wonderful, I know that full well." (Psalm 139:14)

God knows each one of us individually, our purpose, and who we were created to be. He's passionate about restoring what's missing from our lives, redeeming lost time, and turning us into the image of Jesus. My prayer is that you'll allow our heavenly Father to show you in His Word who He says you are. You'll never be the same!

I've been reading *The Forgotten Way* by Ted Dekker, who's an amazing author. He wrote a series of meditations in this book, and his conclusion is that, "It's all about identity."

Who am I ... Really? You and I live to discover the answer to that question. When we do, we'll comprehend that we're far more valuable than we've ever imagined! This is our healing ... to see and live who we truly are.

A Fairytale Rescue

My last chapter describes a most amazing journey, the beginning of a fabulous relationship with my heavenly Father, and how I found true love at last! His love is unconditional, never ending, and embraces an eternal happily ever after! I invite you to my "Fairytale Rescue" in Chapter 11 ... knowing that the same ending is available to you!

Chapter 11

Fairytale Rescue

To rescue: Save from a dangerous or distressing situation ... an act of being rescued from danger. To be free from confinement, danger or evil, save and deliver.

FROM THE TIME YOU AND I WERE BORN, we've been in and were educated by the world's system. We were born with a love deficit, and we were separated from God. Jesus came into this world to bring us into right relationship with our heavenly Father, our Creator. Until we are "born again", we're like sponges trying to soak up whatever we can from those around us, yet we're still not satisfied.

For those of you who have been looking to people, church, jobs, kids, or material things to love you and/or make you feel good about yourself, I just want you to know, it'll wear you out!

I've been a believer since 1979, but I really didn't comprehend what took place at the cross of Calvary. Unfortunately, I never encountered unconditional love, until I invited Jesus into my heart, and I never fully understood that the God of the universe created me to be in relationship with Him, so that I might know Him and experience His love.

As I was being transformed into His image, I received His love, and I could be His love to a lost and dying world! This has been a mind-blowing reality … and it's the Gospel! As I've been meditating on "Christ in me", and believing it, my entire view of life is changing.

God's Love

When you ask God to teach you about His love, and how He wants us to love others, the answer is provided in Matthew 22:37-39, where Jesus says, *"Love the Lord your God with all your heart, soul, and mind. This is the first and greatest commandment. The second most important is similar: Love your neighbor as you love yourself."* Jesus further explained, *"Your strong love for each other will prove to the world that you are my disciples."* (John 13:35 *TLB*)

My quest has always been to find out where I belonged and who would love me. I had no sense of identity or who I was meant to be. Take some time to begin discovering your identity, value, and purpose. We were created for love and to be loved. God rescued me first from myself, and then from my dependence upon others! It took time before I could just sit with the Lord, so we could be together, and read my Bible. As I read His words, I became like a little child, and I experienced my fairytale rescue. It's not as I thought it would be … it was better!

Unconditional, Never-Ending Love

God is my Father and His unconditional love has healed and strengthened me. I'm now able to look around me and see … really see people, their value, and worth. God loves through me now, so I don't have to wonder if they're going to love me back … all of that has gone away!

God wants to give you abundant life, and I really do hope you'll believe that! I don't want you to have to go around as many mountains as I did, before I finally, fully surrendered to God and His truths. God is love and He never gives up on us! He knew me and loved me even when I was fighting against him, while I was doing my own thing, and I was in a reckless and broken state. It has been an amazing, life-giving, and transforming experience!

It's so easy to tell someone you love them, so that you can use them, and I was used so many times! I was so desperate for love that I believed what I was told, even if it was just for a little while. I promise you that God isn't like anyone who has ever disappointed or rejected you. He can be trusted with your heart!

My heart's desire for this book is that you might be drawn into the Father heart of God, and perhaps for the first time ever, you'll taste His unconditional, never-ending love. You'll never go back, I promise! Your fairytale rescue starts when you say "Yes" to God, and a magnificent relationship with your heavenly Father begins! It's your happily ever after … God will never change His heart or mind about His great love for you!

Helpful Resources

- *www.Bethel.org* (Worship music and resources)
- *www.compassionatefriends.org* (Support group for the loss of a child at any age)
- *www.griefshare.org* (Support group after the loss of loved one)
- *www.ihopkc.org* (Resources and prayer support at the International House of Prayer, Kansas City)
- *www.mooseheart.org* (For information about my childhood home)
- *www.royalfamilykids.org* (Help sponsor and send a foster child to camp)
- *www.savethestorks.com* (Help for abortion-vulnerable women; mobile van with ultrasound is available)

Ministries

- Dan Mohler (Messages on Neck Ministries: *www.neckministries.com*, also on YouTube)
- Joyce Meyer Ministries (*www.joycemeyer.org*, also on YouTube)
- Patricia King Ministries (*www.patriciakingministries.com*, also on YouTube)

Books

- *Empty Arms: Hope and Support for Those Who Have Suffered a Miscarriage, Stillbirth, or Tubal Pregnancy* by Pam Vredevelt
- *Good Grief* by Granger E. Westberg
- *I Do Again: How We Found a Second Chance at Our Marriage —and You Can Too* by Cheryl and Jeff Scruggs
- *I'll Hold You in Heaven* by Jack Hayford
- *The Art of Forgiving: When You Need to Forgive and Don't Know How* by Lewis B. Smedes
- *The Art of Helping: What to Say and Do When Someone is Hurting* by Lauren Littauer Briggs
- *The Passion Translation New Testament: With Psalms, Proverbs and Song of Songs* by Dr. Brian Simmons
- *Unplanned: The Dramatic True Story of a Former Planned Parenthood Leader's Eye-Opening Journey Across the Life Line* by Abby Johnson
- *What Grieving People Wish You Knew about What Really Helps (and What Really Hurts)* by Nancy Guthrie
- *Where Do Broken Hearts Go? Healing and Hope After Abortion* by Jane Abbate

About the Author

Debbie Forney is a speaker, author, and encourager. Within her heart, she carries one great desire ... that people would know the depths of God's great love for them! She lives in Florida with her husband Ron, and her daughter Laura, not too far away.

Contact Information:

debbieforneyinfo@gmail.com
www.debbieforney.com